BIRDS
BILLS & MOUTHS

FAUN

BIRDS
BILLS & MOUTHS

Jack B. Kochan

STACKPOLE
BOOKS

Published by
STACKPOLE BOOKS
5067 Ritter Road
Mechanicsburg, PA 17055

Printed in the United States of America

10 9 8 7 6 5 4 3 2 1

First edition

Cover design by Caroline Miller and Tina Marie Hill

Library of Congress Cataloging-in-Publication Data

Kochan, Jack B.
    Bills & mouths / Jack B. Kochan.
       p.   cm.—(Birds)
    Includes bibliographical references.
    ISBN 0-8117-3057-3
    1. Wood-carving.   2. Bill (Anatomy).   3. Birds in art.   4. Birds—Anatomy.
    I. Title.   II. Title: Bills and mouths.   II. Series: Kochan, Jack B. Birds.
TT199.7.K628   1995
731'.832—dc20
                                              95-3235
                                                CIP

This book is dedicated to the many wildlife photographers throughout the world. Without their diligent efforts there would be very few reference materials available for carvers, artists, or wildlife enthusiasts. The art of wildlife photography is painstaking, tiring, frustrating, and at times dangerous. Wildlife photography requires a unique breed of person who deserves a special "thank you."

Contents

Preface

The bill is, perhaps, the most outstanding feature on the head of any bird. The bill is often the main means of recognition of a species and is nearly always a primary identifying feature for cataloging a species into a family. With so much information about bills available, it is surprising to find how little the artist and carver really know about this part of a bird.

Most artists are aware of the basic bill shape of the species being portrayed, but they often neglect a detail or two necessary for accuracy. Carvers, in general, seem to be better informed, but they too are often lacking in full understanding of the bill. There seems to be the attitude that the only knowledge necessary is to know what a bill looks like on the surface. Many carvers can produce fine replicas of a bill by referring to castings or photographs. Their accuracy and ability falls short, however, when the bill is portrayed in an open position and the inside of the mouth is exposed.

Only a handful of carvers and artists know what the inside of a bird's mouth looks like. It is with this thought in mind that this book is being written. Every attempt will be made to illustrate and describe every aspect of a bird's bill and mouth. This knowledge will, I hope, aid every carver and artist to better portray our feathered friends.

The material contained in this volume has been compiled from many ornithological texts and personal studies. Since much of the information is of a technical nature, this book also becomes a good reference source for the ornithology student.

The topography of a bill showing the various parts.

ONE

Topography

The bill, or rostrum, of a bird is basically a two-part structure comprised of the upper mandible, or maxilla, and the lower mandible. The two parts, collectively, are called the ramus. The longitudinal centerline ridge of the upper mandible is the culmen, which extends from the tip of the upper mandible to the bases of the

feathers on the forehead. The cutting edges of the upper mandible are called the upper mandibular tomia (singular is tomium). Near the base, on each side of the upper mandible are the nostrils or nares. On most small songbirds the nostril opens into a depression called the nasal fossa.

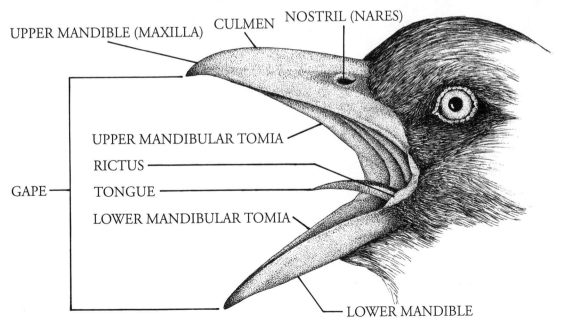

UPPER MANDIBLE (MAXILLA) — CULMEN — NOSTRIL (NARES)

UPPER MANDIBULAR TOMIA

RICTUS

GAPE

TONGUE

LOWER MANDIBULAR TOMIA

LOWER MANDIBLE

1

The lower mandible also has cutting edges called the lower mandibular tomia. When the bill is closed, the tomia of the lower mandible are overlapped slightly by the tomia of the upper mandible. The line formed where the closed upper and lower mandibles meet is called the commissure. The gape is a term sometimes used for the commissure, but the gape usually refers to the space of the open mouth, between the upper and lower mandibles. The tomium has two parts. The hard cutting edge is the tomium proper. The posterior point where the upper and lower mandibles join, at the corners of the mouth, is a soft fleshy area called the rictus.

The longitudinal centerline ridge on the ventral side of the lower mandible is the gonys. When viewed from the ventral, or bottom side, the lower mandible has a pronglike projection on each side. This is the mandibular ramus. Where the lower mandible forms a joint with the quadrate bone is the angle of the jaw. The feathered area in the V of the mandibular ramus is the chin. Directly posterior of the chin is the gular region.

Covering the nostrils of the common pigeon, doves, and a few other species is a fleshy growth called the operculum. Similar to the operculum is the cere, which in many cases is as hard as the bill itself and is seen on hawks, falcons, and several other species. The terms operculum and cere are often used interchangeably to refer to the same thing even though there is a slight difference. The term operculum is taken from Latin and means *lid*, while cere, also from Latin, means *wax*, because it looks waxy.

On ducks and geese there is a hard protrusion at the tip of the upper mandible called the unguis, but it is more commonly known as the nail. Pelicans and many other waterbirds also have a nail.

TWO

Skeletal Structure

The skeletal structure of a bird's head can be divided into three basic groups of bones. The first group is the bones that make up the cranium, or brain enclosure, and the orbits. These bones collectively are called the skull. These are fully described in the second volume in this series, and therefore will not be discussed here.

A second group of bones are those of the face that primarily make up the skeleton of the upper and lower mandibles. There are more than a dozen separate bones that form the skeletal structure of a bird's bill. The upper mandible is made up of many separate bones that have fused into one structure called the maxilla. The premaxillae are the left and right halves that form the tip of the upper mandible called the premaxilla. Each half of the premaxilla has three rearward projecting parts or processes. On the dorsal or top side of the bill, the projecting processes of the premaxilla continue to the frontals of the skull and are called the nasal process. The nasal processes are fused along their centerline to form the culmen, or centerline ridge, of the bill.

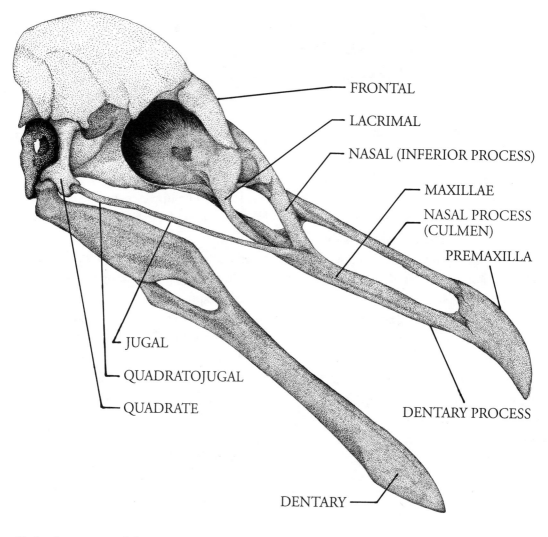

FRONTAL

LACRIMAL

NASAL (INFERIOR PROCESS)

MAXILLAE

NASAL PROCESS
(CULMEN)

PREMAXILLA

JUGAL

QUADRATOJUGAL

QUADRATE

DENTARY PROCESS

DENTARY

*Skeletal structure of the upper
and lower mandible.*

A second projection of the premaxilla, called the dentary process, extends to each side of the upper mandible and forms one-half of the tomium, or cutting edge, on each side of the upper mandible. The dentary processes join with the two maxillae bones to complete the tomia. The third projection of the premaxilla is the palatal process, which extends rearward on the ventral, or underside, along the roof of the mouth and joins with the palatines. The palatines are a pair of bones forming the palate or roof of the mouth.

Skeletal structure of the palate, or roof of the mouth.

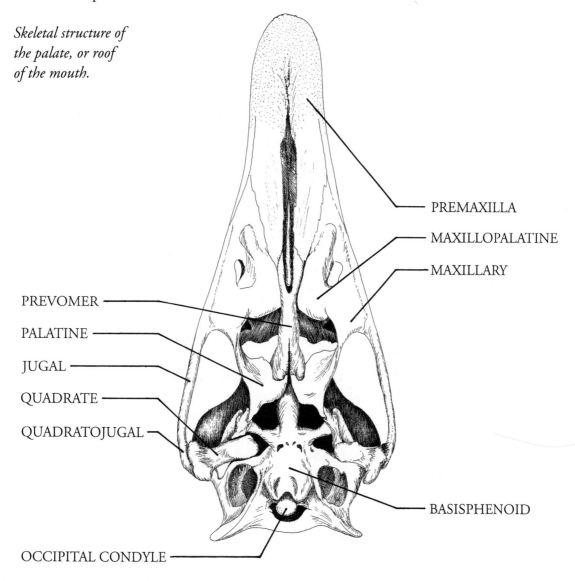

PREMAXILLA

MAXILLOPALATINE

MAXILLARY

PREVOMER

PALATINE

JUGAL

QUADRATE

QUADRATOJUGAL

BASISPHENOID

OCCIPITAL CONDYLE

The maxillae are a pair of bones that form the left and right tomium of the upper mandible. The anterior, or front end, of each maxilla is fused to the dentary processes of the premaxilla while the posterior, or rearward, ends are sutured to the jugals. The jugal bones—one on each side of the bill—are rather slender and are fused to the also slender quadratojugals. The jugals and quadratojugals together make up the zygomatic bar on each side of the upper mandible. The posterior, or rearward, end of the zygomatic bar forms an articulated joint with the quadrate bone.

The posterior ends of each maxilla have a somewhat flattened projection that extends downward and inward to form the roof of the mouth and are known as the ventral processes. The two ventral processes do not meet, thus creating a cleft or slitlike opening in the roof of the mouth. In humans the ventral processes join together to form a single bone for holding the teeth of the upper jaw.

The front ends of the palatines are fused to the maxillae, while the posterior ends form an articulated joint with the pterygoids.

The upper mandible is attached to the frontal by a membrane that creates a moveable hinge. This hinge allows the upper mandible to articulate slightly with the cranium by a process known as cranial kinesis. Kinesis is movement caused by external forces such as biting, rather than by muscle action. The amount of movement varies greatly between species depending upon their feeding habits. In fruit-eating birds such as parrots, the movement is very pronounced, but it is greatly reduced in birds like the ostrich that must bite off the grass they eat. The nasals are a pair of bones that form the outer margins of the left and right nasal cavities.

The lower mandible is made up of ten separate bones—five on each side—that are fused into one rigid, V-shaped structure. In a few species, and most very young birds, these bones are moveable with respect to each other and provide the ability for the lower mandible to widen as the mouth is opened. This allows for the intake of larger pieces of food that the bird could otherwise not eat. As the young bird matures, these bones fuse together, creating a more rigid structure. The centerline ridge on the ventral, or underside, where the left and right halves of the lower mandible are fused together is called the gonys.

The posterior ends of the forked lower mandible form articulated joints with the lower ends of the two quadrate bones. This joint becomes the angle of the jaw. It is this joint where the lower jaw articulates, or pivots, when the mouth is opened. This joint is well below and behind the orbit, or eye socket. When carving or drawing an open-mouthed bird, the artist must remember the pivot point at the angle of the jaw.

The third group of bones in the head are those of the tongue and mouth. All the bones of the tongue collectively form the hyoid apparatus, which can be divided into two groups. The median or "middle" group contains the glossohyal, which is the skeleton for the bulk of the tongue. At the posterior end of the glossohyal is the basihyal.

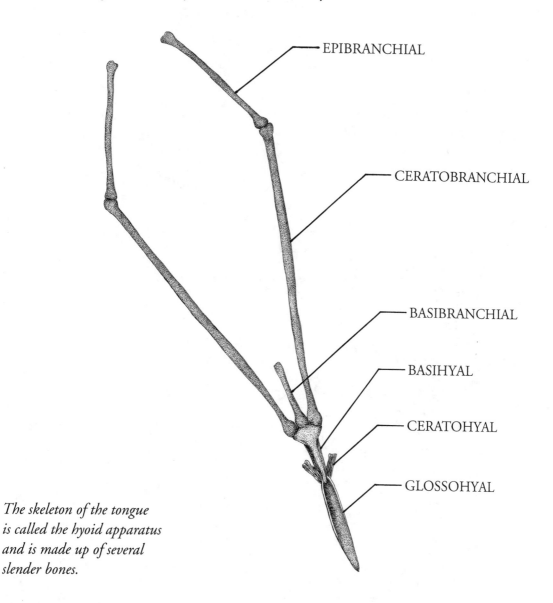

EPIBRANCHIAL

CERATOBRANCHIAL

BASIBRANCHIAL

BASIHYAL

CERATOHYAL

GLOSSOHYAL

The skeleton of the tongue is called the hyoid apparatus and is made up of several slender bones.

Branching off the sides of the basihyal are the horns of the hyoid apparatus. These horns are made up of two pairs of very slender bones. The first pair of slender bones, attached to the basihyal, are the ceratobranchials, which form an articulated joint at their posterior end with the epibranchials.

The hyoid apparatus of the woodpecker is highly developed and, along with the attached muscles, becomes a mechanism that allows extreme extension and retraction of the tongue. With this ability the woodpecker can collect insects in the holes of trees.

The hyoid apparatus of a woodpecker allows for extreme extension of the tongue. The horns and muscles of the hyoid encircle the skull and terminate near the right nostril.

HYOID APPARATUS INSERTS
NEAR RIGHT NOSTRIL

GENIOHYOID ORIGINATES

BASE OF TONGUE

GENIOHYOID MUSCLE

The bones of all birds are highly pneumatized, having many air cavities. This makes them very lightweight but quite strong. The strength comes from the mechanical structure and shape of these air cavities. In the bill, and other bones, the structure resembles the trusses of a bridge. This bone structure of the bill varies slightly between species depending on their feeding habits.

Cross section of a crow's bill shows the trusslike structure of the bones. This pneumatic structure makes the bill lightweight, yet very strong.

Birds that crack open seeds or nuts for food have extra reinforcement around the area where the seed is placed for shelling. Birds that tear apart their food, such as vultures, have additional structural reinforcement near the tip of the bill; in some cases, this area is nearly solid bone.

Woodpeckers have yet another design that helps absorb the shock when they are pecking a tree in search of food; the frontals of a woodpecker are heavier than in most other birds. Additional cartilage between moveable joints is yet another means of shock absorption.

Ornithologists, biologists, and scientists have made extensive studies of the bone structure of bills, and much information is available. The forces and stresses on the various parts of the bill can be calculated mathematically, the same way an engineer can calculate the stresses when designing a bridge.

THREE

Covering

The integument, or covering, on all animals and birds consists of the hair, skin, scales, and feathers. The integument is divided into two main layers: the dermis, or underlayer, and the epidermis, or surface layer. The integument of the ramus, or bill, is a durable horny sheath called the ramphotheca.

In most birds the ramphotheca is quite hard, and corneous (from the Latin for *horn*) but it is of a leathery texture, except at the tip, in flamingos and ducks. In some birds that probe the ground for food, such as the woodcock, snipe, and some shorebirds, the ramphotheca is softer at the tip of the upper mandible.

For the most part, the ramphotheca follows the contour of the skeletal structure of the bill and is bound to the bones by elastic fibers. In many species there are areas of thickening of the ramphotheca that create a different surface appearance. Ridges, ripples, and grooves appear on the bills of many ducks, and swans have a knobby growth on the upper mandible. Just before mating season, the male pelican grows a protrusion on the upper mandible that helps protect the soft pouch when fighting with other pelicans during courtship battles. This protrusion disappears after the bird acquires a mate.

The base, or proximal end, of the upper mandible ramphotheca is often modified by being softer and thicker. This thickening creates the cere or operculum. In parrots the cere is partly feathered, but in hawks, falcons, and owls it is bare and often brightly colored.

The horny ramphotheca is constantly being worn away by abrasion from use and is continuously being restored, or keratinized, from beneath the surface. In most birds the tip of the bill wears away from use, especially by birds that feed on the ground, such as quail and pheasants. Renewing the ramphotheca occurs continuously toward the tip in the same manner that human fingernails grow. If the bill becomes injured and the mandibles no longer meet properly, the ramphotheca may grow distorted. This distortion could hinder eating and food gathering, often causing the bird to starve to death.

In some species the surface of the ramphotheca is shed either in small, thin sheets or in one piece, as in ptarmigans and some grouse. This shedding generally takes place prior to the time of mating or, in some cases, shortly after mating. In most cases, shedding of the ramphotheca also coincides with molting of the feathers.

While a bird is still an embryo in the egg, a sharp protrusion is formed on the tip of the bill. This protrusion, known as the eggtooth, is used to cut through and open the eggshell for hatching. The eggtooth appears on all species and disappears within a week, or less, after hatching. The eggtooth appears on either the upper or lower mandible, and sometimes on both.

On a few species, the integument contains soft, fleshy growths called caruncles. Caruncles normally appear about the head and neck of a bird. One type of caruncle grows at the corners of the mouth, or rictus, of certain species. These growths are called lappets or rictal wattles. Rictal wattles are extended flaps of skin at the corners of the mouth, as seen in the masked lapwing, and are often brightly colored.

The ramphotheca is well supplied with blood vessels, nerves, and sensory cells called corpuscles. Blood vessels are more abundant in the palate than on the sides of the bill, thus making the mouth lining more reddish in color. Nerve fibers are found in the cere of only a few species. Sensory corpuscles, however, are abundant throughout the ramphotheca of all birds.

There are two types of sensory corpuscles: Herbst and Gandry's. Gandry's corpuscles appear in the bills of ducks and owls, while Herbst corpuscles appear in all bills. Both types are believed to be highly sensitive to vibration and pressure, thus giving the bill an acute sense of touch. Woodcock, snipe, and many shorebirds have an abundant amount of Herbst corpuscles located in the tip of the bill. As these birds probe the soft earth or muddy shoreline in search of food, they can find their prey by touch without seeing it.

Fleshy flaps of skin at the corners of the mouth are called lappets, or rictal wattles, as seen in the masked lapwing.

FOUR

Size and Shape

Ornithologists classify the bill of a bird into more than twenty different categories. With more than nine thousand different species, it is obvious that there are just as many different sizes and shapes.

It is not necessary that the carver learn all these categories, but it should indicate the importance of having good reference materials before starting a carving.

When the bill length is less than the length of the head, the bill is classed as short, as in the junco.

14

Bill shapes are categorized primarily by their external structural characteristics, features, or size and are usually referenced to the features of the upper mandible. The bill of a stork, for example, is markedly longer than the head and is classified as long, whereas the short bill is shorter than the head, as in the junco.

The stork has a bill that is both long and straight.

The curved tip of the upper mandible of hawks, owls, and eagles is longer than the lower mandible and forms the hooked bill. Sometimes the tips of the mandibles overlap each other like a pair of scissors and are classed as crossed, as in the cross-bill. When the upper mandible is higher than it is wide, as in the puffin, it is said to be compressed, whereas a depressed mandible is wider (usually near the tip) than it is high, as seen on most ducks.

The kite has a hooked bill in which the tip of the longer upper mandible curves over the shorter lower mandible.

The tips of a crossed bill overlap like a pair of shears.

The grouse and grosbeak have stout bills that are obviously high and wide. The terete bill of a hummingbird has a cross-sectional shape that is round. When the commissure is in line with the head, the bill is said to be straight as that of the stork. A bill is considered as recurved if the tip curves upward, and decurved if the tip curves down, as seen in the Terek sandpiper and honeyeater respectively. In a few species of hummingbirds, the bill decurves nearly to a half-circle. A bill of this shape is called a sickle bill.

The puffin is the most commonly known bird with a compressed bill, but the belted kingfisher also has a compressed bill that is higher than it is wide over most of its length.

The depressed bill is greatly flattened, usually near the tip, as seen in ducks.

The stout bill of a ring-necked pheasant is obviously high and wide.

A bill is terete when the cross-sectional shape is round, as seen in hummingbirds.

CROSS SECTION AA

The slightly recurved bill of a Terek sandpiper curves upward at the tip.

When the bill curves downward it is classed as decurved, as in the honeyeater.

When the bill is decurved into nearly a half-circle it is called a sickle bill, as in the sicklebill hummingbird.

The bill of a flamingo is deflected at a downward angle, at approximately the midpoint of its length, and is said to be bent. A grosbeak has a mandible with convex sides and is classed as swollen, while the acute bill of the winter wren comes to a very sharp point. The tip of the hairy woodpecker's bill is beveled and is classed as chisel-like.

The bent bill of a flamingo angles sharply downward near its midpoint.

The convex sides of the evening grosbeak's bill classify it as swollen.

The sharply pointed bill of a winter wren is considered to be acute. The nostrils are located in depressions called the nasal fossae.

The beveled tip of a
woodpecker's bill gives it
a chisel-like characteristic.

On a few species, the upper mandible
has an obvious hump, as seen on the
scoter, and is termed gibbous. The north-
ern shoveler has a bill that is depressed and
extremely widened near the tip. This is the
spatulate or spoon-shaped bill.

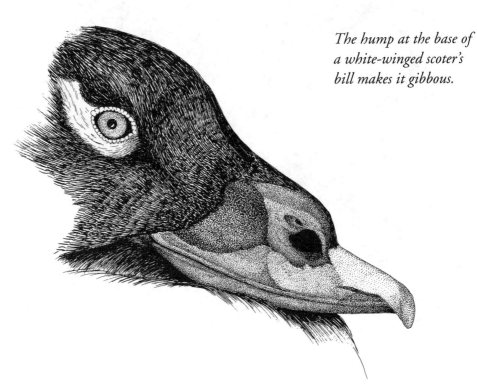

*The hump at the base of
a white-winged scoter's
bill makes it gibbous.*

The spatulate bill is flat and extremely wide, or spoon-shaped, at the tip, as in the spoonbill.

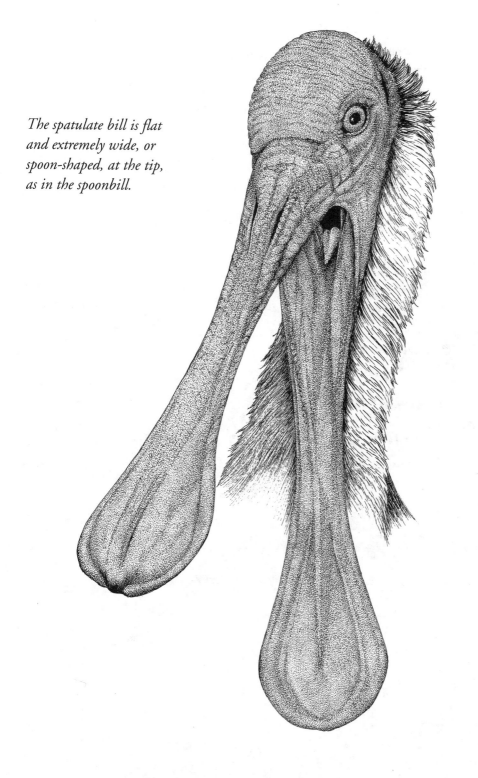

Birds have evolved dramatically since the time of Archeopteryx and no longer have teeth, but some species have what could be construed as teeth. Mergansers have a bill that is classed as serrate. Along the tomia, or cutting edge, of the mandibles are lateral serrations or tooth-like ridges.

Toothlike serrations on the tomia of a merganser give it a bill that is serrate.

Ducks and other water birds have lateral ridges along the tomia, creating the lamellate, or sieve-bill, as seen on the shoveler.

Ducks, geese, and swans have similar "teeth" and are said to have a bill that is lamellate or sieve-billed. When the tomia has a toothlike nick, usually near the tip, the bill is notched. This notch usually occurs on the upper mandible, as seen on thrushes and falcons. (Hawks do not have this notch.) Another shape is the conical, where the bill is quite short and cone shaped, as in the redpoll.

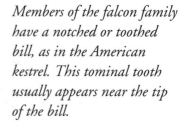

Members of the falcon family have a notched or toothed bill, as in the American kestrel. This tominal tooth usually appears near the tip of the bill.

The cone-shaped bill of a redpoll is said to be conical.

There are several other external characteristics of the bill that help an ornithologist to catalog or classify a species. The bill with an angulated commissure has a commissure line that is bent at the point where the tomia meets the rictus, as seen in grosbeaks and finches. Pelicans and cormorants have a bill with a gular sac. In pelicans, this is a conspicuous, unfeathered, fleshy sac or pouch, on the ventral side of the lower mandible in the gular region. In the cormorant it is not so conspicuous and is partially feathered.

The commissure line of the red-winged blackbird bends downward near the rictus. This is a bill with an angulated commissure.

Pelicans, cormorants, and other seabirds have a pouch or gular sac on the lower mandible. This is a white pelican.

As with almost any subject, bill shapes also have exceptions. A few species exist in the world that do not fit well into the common categories of bill shapes. The shoebill of Africa is one of these species. The shoebill has a bill that is extremely high and wide. The zygomatic bar and lower jawbone are obviously wider than the skull, thus creating the appearance of a very large head. The upper mandible is slightly hooked at the tip where a nail also appears.

The shoebill of Africa has a bill that is wider at the base than the width of its head.

Variations of the nostrils also play an important role when an ornithologist catalogs a species. The nostrils of a bird are usually separated from each other by a bony wall called the nasal septum, and are referred to as being imperforate. In a few species, such as the vulture, the nostrils do not have the dividing septum. You can literally see through one nostril and out the other, and is therefore called perforate.

When there is no nasal septum, the nostrils are said to be perforate. In the turkey vulture you can see in one nostril and out the other.

The common pigeon has a fleshy cere, or operculum, that extends partly over the nostril openings. This operculate characteristic of the nostrils is apparent in most doves, hawks, and falcons. Normally the operculum is fleshy and softer than the surrounding ramphotheca but, in some species, it is membranous and nearly as hard as the bill itself, as seen in the barn swallow.

Any single species could, and usually does, have two or more of these external characteristics. A falcon, for example, has a hooked and notched bill with a cere. Ducks have a depressed, lamellate bill with a nail. The bent bill of a flamingo is also lamellate, and the terete bill of the hummingbird is also obviously long. You can readily see that there can be many characteristic combinations.

Measurements of the bill are nearly always taken by ornithologists when doing studies on any species. Along with many other measurements, these are an asset in evaluating differences between species, sexes of the same species, and growth of a particular species. Measurements are also used to help determine regional variations of a species, which usually are caused by dietary differences. The bill measurement is taken on the upper mandible from the tip to the posterior end of the culmen where it meets the forehead.

On hawks, eagles, and other species that have a cere, the measurement is made from the tip of the bill to the midline point at the front edge of the cere. Bill measurement is always a straight line, even if the bill is curved.

The size of a bill is not related to the overall size of a bird. Relatively small birds could have extremely large bills, as seen in toucans, and large birds could have relatively small bills, as seen in the rhea and ostrich.

Bill size and shape do relate, however, to the feeding habits of all birds. Species that probe the ground with their bills in search of food usually have rather long, slender bills. The hooked tip on the bill of a hawk or vulture is used to tear apart the flesh of the prey or carrion.

Fish-eating birds, such as mergansers, have toothlike serrations along the tomia to help hold their catch while the gular sac of pelicans becomes a "scoop" for obtaining their supply of aquatic food. The lamellate bills of flamingos and ducks become devices for straining edible grasses and organisms included in their diet.

FIVE

Nostrils

The shape of the nostril openings, or nares (pronounced NAY-reez), is also a determining factor when classifying a species. The nostrils of a killdeer are linear in shape, forming a narrow line or slitlike opening, while accipiters, such as the red-tail hawk, have an oval or teardrop-shaped nostril opening. Falcons have a circular or rounded nostril opening. Members of the shearwater family and albatrosses have a special tubular structure on the bill from the nares to the nasal cavity and are called tubenoses.

The long slitlike nostrils of a killdeer are considered linear.

The white-capped albatross
has a tubelike structure from
the nares to the nasal cavity
and so is called a tubenose.

The bald eagle has
oval nostrils that are
positioned nearly
perpendicular to the
commissure line.

*Falcons have a
round nostril with a bony
tubercle growing just inside the opening.*

The nostrils of most species have some means of protection surrounding them. Crows, for example, are carrion eaters and have rather heavy feathering covering the nares. This feathering protects the nostril from becoming clogged with bits of meat when the bird places its bill into a carcass to eat. The ramphotheca surrounding the nares of most fast-flying birds of prey is raised or rippled. This raised area becomes a deflector that changes the air flow over the nostril when the bird is in a high-speed dive in pursuit of prey. Without this deflective mechanism, a partial vacuum could be created at the nostril and breathing would be difficult or impossible. Falcons have yet another airflow deflector. A bony protuberance called a tubercle is in the center of the nostril opening. As previously mentioned, pigeons and doves have fleshy operculums that protect their nostril openings.

In nearly all birds the nostrils are pervious, or open. In adult cormorants, gannets, and anhingas, however, the nostrils are closed by bone or are completely missing. Such a nostril is said to be impervious. It is assumed, therefore, that these birds must breathe through their mouths. Cormorants and gannets, however, have a permanently open slit at the rictus, or corner of the mouth, that allows them to breathe without opening the jaws. The slit is protected by a fleshy lid that closes when the bird dives under water.

The nostrils open into the nasal cavity, which is located just above the palate of the mouth. Inside the nasal cavity are three pairs of thin, scroll-like linings called conchae. The conchae are usually covered with a moist mucous membrane that traps dust and helps to warm the air being breathed. The clean, warm air leaves the nasal cavity and enters the mouth, then the glottis, in its passage to the lungs and air sacs. It is within the conchae that the olfactory nerves, which are the sensors of smell, originate.

Nearly all birds have olfactory organs, but only a few species have a keen sense of smell. The kiwi probably has the keenest sense of smell of any bird. With nostrils near the tip of the bill, large nasal cavities, and well-developed conchae, the kiwi has an olfactory system much like a mammal. This elaborate system allows the bird to search for food by smell, since the kiwi has very poor vision. Vultures also locate their food mainly by smell. In birds with impervious, or closed, nostrils such as the cormorant, odors are transmitted to the olfactory nerve through the mouth.

The nares are not located at the same relative point on all species. In most cases the nares are located close to the base of the upper mandible on each side of the culmen. In some species the nares are closer to the longitudinal midpoint of the mandible, while a few species, such as the kiwi, have the nostril openings closer to the tip. Good reference material is a definite necessity when producing a carving or creating a painting of any wildfowl.

Castings of bills are an excellent reference, as are study skins and some taxidermy mounts. Recent practices in taxidermy, however, have included the use of castings to replace the real bill on some birds and may not be an accurate replica of the original bill.

Bill size, bill shape, and nostril shape are the primary factors considered when an ornithologist classifies a bird into a particular family, subfamily, species, or subspecies. The following chart shows the various bill characteristics of most bird families. Surface characteristics of the bill, however, are not the only means an ornithologist uses for classifying a bird. Differences in the structure of the palate, or roof of the mouth, is also used to help catalog a species. These structural differences are described in chapter 7.

BILL CHARACTERISTICS OF BIRD FAMILIES

Albatross (Diomedeidae)
Bill: Long; straight; hooked at tip.
Nostril: Very small; tubular, opening into separate tubes.

Anhinga (Anhingidae)
Bill: Long; straight; acute; gular sac (medium).
Nostril: Very small.

Avocet and Stilt (Recurvirostridae)
Bill: Long; slender; recurved.
Nostril: Linear.

Blackbird and Oriole (Icterinae)
Bill: Length varies with species; conical; acute; elevated at base and extending far back into the forehead; angulated commissure.
Nostrils: Oval; unfeathered.

Bushtit (Aegithalidae)
Bill: Very short; compressed.
Nostrils: Oval; imperforate.

Cardinal and Grosbeak (Cardinalinae)
Bill: Short; stout; conical; slightly swollen; lower mandibular tomia rolled inward.
Nostrils: Oval, nearly triangular; imperforate.

Cormorant (Phalacrocoracidae)
Bill: As long as head; straight; hooked; gular sac (small).
Nostrils: Absent (impervious).

Crane (Gruidae)
Bill: As long as, or longer than head; straight; compressed.
Nostrils: Preforate.

Creeper (Certhiidae)
Bill: Length varies with species; slender; decurved; compressed.
Nostrils: Oval; imperforate; unfeathered.

Crow and Jay (Corvidae)
Bill: Long; stout; culmen decurved at tip; slightly acute.
Nostrils: Oval; imperforate; sometimes feathered.

Cuckoo and Roadrunner (Cuculidae)
Bill: Size varies with species; usually compressed; slightly decurved.
Nostrils: Oval, almost linear.

Dipper (Cinclidae)
Bill: Short; straight; slender; compressed; notched; culmen decurved at tip; gonys recurved at tip.
Nostrils: Imperforate.

Dove and Pigeon (Columbidae)
Bill: Short; slender; culmen decurved; operculate.
Nostrils: Linear; imperforate; overlapped by operculum.

Duck (Anatidae)
Bill: Either lamellate or serrate, compressed or depressed, with a nail; mergansers have a terrete bill.
Nostrils: Usually oval.

Eagle, Hawk, and Kite (subfamily Accipitrinae)
Bill: Strongly hooked; cere.
Nostrils: Usually oval, with forward end higher; sometimes linear; imperforate.

Falcon (Falconidae)
Bill: Strongly hooked; notched; cere.
Nostrils: Round with central bony tubercle; imperforate.

Finch and Grosbeak (Fringillidae)
Bill: Short; stout; conical; angulated commissure; culmen decurved.
Nostrils: Oval; imperforate.

Flamingo (Phoenicopteridae)
Bill: Long; bent; lamellate.
Nostrils: Linear.

Flycatcher (Tyrannidae)
Bill: Size varies with species; straight; depressed at base; slightly hooked; culmen decurved at tip.
Nostrils: Round; imperforate.

Frigate bird (Fregatidae)
Bill: Long; straight; hooked.
Nostrils: Small; linear.

Gannet (Sulidae)
Bill: Slightly longer than head; straight; decurved at tip; gular sac (small).
Nostrils: Absent.

Goatsucker (Caprimulgidae)
Bill: Short, small, and weak; depressed; hooked; gape is very wide.
Nostrils: Round; sometimes tubular.

Goose (subfamily Anserinae)
Note: Geese are in the family Anatidae, along with ducks and swans.
  Bill: Lamellate; compressed at base and narrowing at tip; some species have a frontal shield.
  Nostrils: Oval.
Grouse and Ptarmigan (Tetraoninae)
  Bill: Stout; short.
  Nostrils: Oval; feathered.
Gull (Laridae)
  Bill: Hooked; straight.
  Nostrils: Linear; perforate.
Heron and Bittern (Ardeidae)
  Bill: Straight; acute.
  Nostrils: Oval; nearly linear; lores usually bare.
Horned Lark (Alaudidae)
  Bill: Short; conical; acute.
  Nostrils: Oval; concealed by feather tufts.
Hummingbird (Trochilidae)
  Bill: Slender, and variable in length; terete; straight; sometimes decurved.
  Nostrils: Sometimes partially concealed with feathers.
Ibis (Threskiornithidae)
  Bill: Long; decurved; slender; terete.
  Nostrils: Linear.
Jacana (Jacanidae)
  Bill: As long as head; straight; compressed; frontal shield.
  Nostrils: Oval; nearly linear.
Kingfisher (Alcedinidae)
  Bill: Long; straight; compressed; acute.
  Nostrils: Linear.
Limpkin (Aramidae)
  Bill: Long; compressed; decurved at tip.
  Nostrils: Perforate.
Loon (Gaviidae)
  Bill: Straight; acute; compressed.
  Nostrils: Oval.
Merganser and Eider (Tribe Mergini)
  Bill: Somewhat compressed; terete and serrate in mergansers; slightly depressed and lamellate in eiders.
  Nostrils: Oval.
Nuthatch (Sittidae)
  Bill: As long as head; straight; slender; compressed; acute; gonys recurved at tip.
  Nostrils: Oval; imperforate.

Osprey (Pandioninae)
  Bill: Hooked; cere.
  Nostrils: Oval; imperforate.
Owl (Strigidae)
Note: Barn owl is in the family Tytonidae.
  Bill: Hooked; culmen decurved; cere.
  Nostrils: Oval; at edge of cere.
Oystercatcher (Haematopodidae)
  Bill: Long; straight; compressed; chisel-like.
  Nostrils: Oval; nearly linear.
Parrot and Macaw (Psittacidae)
  Bill: Short; stout; culmen strongly decurved; hooked; cere.
  Nostrils: Round; imperforate.
Pelican (Pelecanidae)
  Bill: Very long; straight; hooked; gular sac (large).
  Nostrils: Absent.
Pheasant (Phasianinae)
  Bill: Short; stout; culmen decurved; tip of upper mandible bent over lower mandible.
  Nostrils: Oval; imperforate.
Plover (Charadriidae)
  Bill: Constricted in middle and swollen at tip.
  Nostrils: Oval.
Puffin and Auk (Alcidae)
  Bill: Varies in shape and length; greatly compressed in puffins.
  Nostrils: Imperforate.
Quail (Odontophorinae)
  Bill: Short; stout; culmen decurved; finely serrated.
  Nostrils: Oval; imperforate.
Rail and Coot (Rallidae)
  Bill: Varies in length and shape with species.
  Nostrils: Perforate.
Sandpiper and Woodcock (Scolopacidae)
  Bill: Varies in length with species; slender; pliable at tip; tip somewhat depressed, or tapering to acute.
  Nostrils: Oval.
Shearwater and Fulmar (Procellariidae)
  Bill: Hooked.
  Nostrils: Tubular, on culmen; imperforate.
Shrike (Laniidae)
  Bill: Short; compressed; hooked; notched.
  Nostrils: Imperforate.

Skimmer (Rynchopinae)
Bill: Straight; compressed very thin; lower mandible considerably longer than upper mandible and blunt at tip.
Nostrils: Perforate.

Skua and Jaeger (Stercorariinae)
Bill: Nail-like hook; cere.
Nostrils: Perforate.

Sparrow (Passeridae) Old World.
Bill: Short; conical; culmen slightly decurved; angulated commissure.
Nostrils: Oval; imperforate.

Spoonbill (Threskiornithidae)
Bill: Straight; broad; spatulate.
Nostrils: Oval.

Starling (Sturnidae)
Bill: As long as head; straight; angulated commissure.
Nostrils: Oval; imperforate.

Storm petrel (Hydrobatidae)
Bill: Hooked; tubenose.
Nostrils: On culmen, united in one tube.

Swallow (Hirundinidae)
Bill: Short; wide at base (triangular in shape); slightly hooked; gape is wide.
Nostrils: Imperforate.

Swan (Tribe Cygnini)
Note: Swans are in the family Anatidae, along with ducks and geese.
Bill: Lamellate; compressed at base; nail; lores bare.
Nostrils: Oval.

Swift (Apodidae)
Bill: Very short; culmen decurved; depressed; wide gape.
Nostrils: Oval.

Tanager (Thraupidae)
Bill: As long as head; conical; stout; swollen; slightly hooked; notched at tip; toothed at middle of upper tomium.
Nostrils: Imperforate; unfeathered.

Tern (Sterninae)
Bill: Short; straight; sometimes acute.
Nostrils: Perforate.

Thrasher and Mockingbird (Mimidae)
Bill: Length varies with species; decurved at tip; notched at tip.
Nostrils: Imperforate.

Thrush (Turdinae)
Bill: Length varies with species, usually short; straight; slender; compressed; culmen decurved at tip; notched at tip.
Nostrils: Imperforate.

Titmouse (Paridae)
Bill: Short; straight; stout; compressed.
Nostrils: Oval; imperforate.

Trogon (Trogonidae)
Bill: Short; wide at base; culmen decurved; upper mandible has several "teeth."
Nostrils: Oval; partially covered with feathers.

Tropicbird (Phaethontidae)
Bill: As long as head; straight; compressed; acute; gular sac (very small).
Nostrils: Linear (small).

Turkey (Meleagridinae)
Bill: Short; stout; culmen decurved at tip; snood or leader appears in male.
Nostrils: Unfeathered.

Verdin (Remizidae)
Bill: Short; acute.
Nostrils: Imperforate.

Vulture (Cathardidae) New world.
Bill: Hooked; cere.
Nostrils: Large; oval; perforate.

Waxwing (Bombycillidae)
Bill: Short; stout; straight; slightly hooked; notched at tip; gape wide.
Nostrils: Imperforate.

Wood Warbler (Parulinae)
Bill: Varies in length with species, usually short; straight; compressed; acute.
Nostrils: Oval; imperforate; unfeathered.

Woodpecker (Picidae)
Bill: Straight; strong; usually chisel-like; acute in some species.
Nostrils: Oval; partially feathered.

Wren (Troglodytidae)
Bill: Length varies with species, usually short; decurved; slender; compressed.
Nostrils: Oval; imperforate.

SIX

Special Features

As in other parts of a bird, the bill often has special features or adaptations that are aside from the norm. Located in the skull behind the nasal cavity, close to each eye socket, is a pair of lateral nasal glands, more commonly called "salt glands." Albatrosses, pelicans, and other seabirds have well-developed salt glands. These glands separate the salt from the sea-water that the birds drink. The salt solu-tion is then secreted through the nostrils or the mouth. Petrels will "shoot" the salty fluid out their tubular nostrils, while in other birds it dribbles out the nostrils. In cormorants, where the nostrils are impervi-ous, this salt solution drains into the mouth then flows to the tip of the bill. The solution is disposed of by the shaking of the head, which is a common character-istic movement in most seabirds.

The ramphotheca, or bill covering, on the upper mandible of some species extends up and over the forehead. This frontal shield is seen in coots, geese, and swans.

When the ramphotheca of the upper mandible extends over the forehead, the bird has a frontal shield, as seen in the coot.

The upper mandible ramphotheca sometimes has another special feature called a casque. The casque is a hard, horny growth that appears in several ways. In cassowaries, it is a growth that covers the entire top of the head, while in the rhinoceros hornbill the casque is a large, horny growth that overhangs the upper mandible.

Lappets or rictal wattles, mentioned earlier, are extended flaps of skin that grow from the corners of the mouth. Rictal wattles are found in several species such as the wattled crow, wattled starling, and the lapwing. Rictal wattles are often brightly colored and increase in color intensity during mating season. Ornithologists are still trying to determine the purpose and use of such wattles.

The rhinoceros hornbill has a casque that extends over the upper mandible.

SEVEN

Mouths

At some point in time, nearly every artist or carver will want to portray a species with an open mouth. The open-mouthed position suggests various attitudes of a bird; nestlings waiting to be fed, an adult in song, a defensive posture, or simply a lazy yawn requires an open-mouthed position. This attitude makes the interior of the mouth visible and therefore requires additional knowledge in order to depict it accurately. Good reference material and careful study are essential when portraying an open-mouthed or "gaping" bird. Unfortunately, very little good reference material about the mouth of a bird is available to the artist.

Most of the photography references are those of very young birds waiting to be fed, and these photos can be a very good source of reference. Also available from several suppliers are "two-piece" castings of bills, usually of ducks, that can be separated to see the inside or mouth area of

the bill, including the tongue. Other than these two sources, very little is ever mentioned about the mouth of a bird, except in specific ornithological studies.

The mouth is the cavity, internally, between the upper and lower mandibles and is referred to as the buccal cavity. It extends from the tip of the mandibles to the pharynx and includes the tongue. The pharynx is a posterior continuation of the mouth beginning at the back end of the palatal cleft and becomes the beginning of the alimentary canal. More about the alimentary canal and the digestive system of birds will be included in later volumes of *Birds*. In the middle of the upper part of the pharynx is a slitlike opening that is smaller than, but appears as an extension of, the palatal slit. The pharynx is softer and more muscular than the palate.

The palate, or roof of the mouth, is hard and horny near the tip of the bill and somewhat softer rearward as it extends to become the roof of the pharynx. The palate of a bird resembles the soft palate of most mammals.

A midline slit, or cleft, called the choana divides the palate longitudinally into two palatal folds. These palatal folds have tiny, backward-pointing projections, or papillae, and cover the bottom of the nasal cavity. The cleft palate is a typical characteristic found in all birds. The posterior segment of the palate has an elongated depression that usually conforms to the general shape of the tongue.

The palates of all birds' mouths are similar in construction. The palate, or roof of the mouth, has a centerline slit, or cleft, called the choana. The posterior end is hollowed to the general shape of the tongue. The cleft palate and pharyngeal folds appear in all birds.

The shape of the mouth inside the lower mandible follows the skeletal structure, for the most part, in all birds. The floor of the mouth is created by the skin, or integument, that covers the chin area of the lower mandible. The rather soft mucous membrane lining of the integument, along with muscles, forms the floor of the mouth. The space inside the lower mandible is occupied by the tongue, which in most cases also follows the general skeletal shape.

In a few species, such as pelicans, the soft floor of the mouth is a rather large pouch capable of being greatly enlarged by a stretching of the skin.

Birds do not have a voice box, as humans and other mammals do. In birds, there are two laryngeal folds left and right, that form a slitlike opening called the glottis. The edges of the glottis also have tiny papillae and, unlike mammals, there is no epiglottis or "trapdoor" to protect this opening. When a bird swallows food or drinks water, the glottis is closed and protected by the base of the tongue. Behind the glottis, ventrally, is the larynx, which is the beginning of the trachea, or breathing tube.

The top and bottom walls of the glottis have membranous papillae-covered folds called the dorsal and ventral pharyngeal folds. It is these papillae and pharyngeal folds that help a bird to swallow its food in chunks since there are no teeth to grind it into small pieces.

The majority of birds do not have a soft palate. Pigeons and doves are the exception and have a rather soft mouth, which allows them to drink without lifting their head to swallow as most birds do.

The rictus at the corners of the mouths of very young birds is usually swollen and enlarged, forming what are called oral flanges. Some authorities refer to these swollen areas as rictal flanges. The oral flanges are usually a pale white, but sometimes they are a brighter color than the lining of the mouth. In some instances the oral flanges simply contain a brightly colored spot. The difference in color of the oral flanges is probably a guide to the adult for feeding young birds.

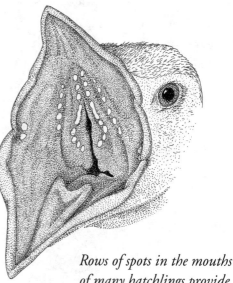

Rows of spots in the mouths of many hatchlings provide a feeding target for the parent bird.

Color patterns other than on the oral flanges of a nestling bird also help to guide the parent while feeding. Strategically placed spots on the palate of a nestling form a "window" for the parent to use as a guide when placing food in the young bird's mouth. These spots are either a brighter or a paler color than the rest of the palate and are known as directive marks.

Mouth spots are not the only means of aiding the parent bird in feeding the young. A young albatross, for example, will face into the breeze with its mouth open in a wide gape. The bright red mouth lining forms a bull's-eye for the feeding target, while the wind-blown downy feathers of the head and neck create a frame around the target.

The bright red mouth lining of a young albatross creates a bulls-eye on the feeding target framed by the dark, wind-blown, downy feathers of the head and neck.

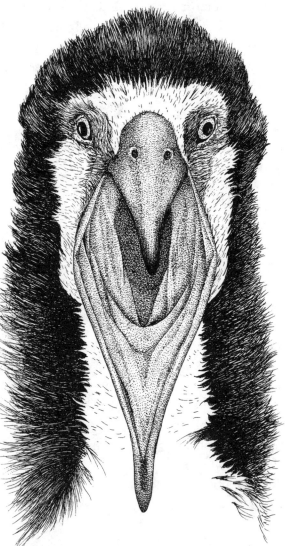

Several species of birds do not place the food into the mouth of the young. The hatchlings of these species are taught to peck for their food. Many of the more than eighty species of gulls, for example, have a brightly colored marking on the bill. This mark appears in the form of a red spot on each side, near the tip, of the lower mandible of the greater black-backed gull, the lesser black-backed gull, and the Thayer's gull. Sabine's gulls have black bills with bright yellow tips. These bright markings are a target for the young gulls to peck at in search of the food that is in the mouth of the parent. This experience teaches the hatchlings to search and peck for their own food.

As mentioned in chapter 4, the bill is a primary means of classifying a species into a family and sometimes an order. Bill shape, size, and external characteristics are not the only factors, however, in the classification of a species. The arrangement of the palatal bones and the general configuration of the inside of the upper mandible also play an important role in classification.

All birds have the ability to emit sounds through the mouth. Different species will sing, cluck, hoot, coo, scream, or warble at different times and for various reasons. Bird song is a study in itself, and though it may be enlightening to the bird enthusiast, it has little significance to the artist.

In humans, sound is produced by vocal cords located in the larynx. Birds, however, have no vocal cords and the sounds a bird makes originate in the syrinx. The syrinx is located at the lower end of the trachea, or breathing tube. In several species of ducks, there is also an additional air sac in the syrinx called a bulla, which is responsible for producing the sounds a male duck makes. In the species that have one, the bulla appears only in the male.

The digestive system of a bird includes the bill lining—or mouth—tongue, salivary glands, pharynx, esophagus, and crop. The remaining internal organs of the digestive system are of little importance to the carver or artist. A part of the digestive system that has some value to the carver and artist, though, is the crop. The crop is a sac of the esophagus, about midpoint in its length. This sac is used to store food, while the bird eats, for later digestion. Not all species have a crop. Some species have what is called a false crop. The false crop is merely an expanded section of the esophagus that performs similar to a crop. The true crop is a sac, or sometimes a pair of sacs (left and right) joined to the esophagus. Most seed eating, or gallinaceous, birds have a crop, as seen in doves and pigeons. It is in the crop that "pigeon milk" is produced. This mucouslike fluid is regurgitated by the parent bird and fed to the very young hatchlings.

When portraying a species that has a crop, thought should be given to the bird's appearance. If the composition depicts the bird as having just eaten, then the crop would be full. The lower front of the neck would have additional fullness, or even a bulge, in the area of the crop.

A few species of birds do not build a nest or even hatch their own eggs. Instead, they will lay their eggs in the nest of another species where the young will be hatched and reared by the "host parent." Species that pursue this behavior are known as "parasite birds." Parasite birds do not randomly select a nest of another species. A parasite will select a particular host species for a place to lay an egg. Normally the parasite's egg will resemble that of the host in size and color. Some species of parasite birds will peck a hole in the eggs of the host bird to assure that only the parasite chick will hatch.

Also, in most cases, the parasite hatchling has the same palatal markings as the host hatchling. These markings deceive the host parent into feeding the parasite hatchling. Palatal spots can vary in color from pale yellow, blue, bright red, or violet to black. Thorough reference photos are an absolute necessity when carving a nest of young birds with gaping mouths. It should also be apparent that a thorough study of the species' habits should be made before starting your carving.

Not all species feed their young after they are hatched. Passerines will bring food to the nest and put the food in the mouth of the young. Gallinaceous birds, such as grouse, teach the young to peck for food. Pecking for food is probably partly instinctive and partly a learned process. Experiments performed with herring gull chicks show that the chick will peck at the red spot on the bill of the parent. The parent gull will then regurgitate food which the chick discovers while pecking. The red spot on the bill of the parent gull gives a point of aim for the chick.

EIGHT

Tongues

Over the years, man has propagated many legends and superstitions about birds. One of these folklore legends is that if you slit the tongue of a crow, it can be taught to talk. This could not be farther from the truth. Although some birds, such as parrots, do imitate human sounds, the splitting of a bird's tongue will not enable it to speak. Such an action would only inflict cruel punishment upon the bird. (A side note: a crow's tongue is already slightly split.)

Folklore and legends throughout Europe and North America indicate that man has held conversations with certain birds. The common phrase "a little bird told me" still exists today.

For the most part, the tongue of a species is adapted in size, shape, texture, sensitivity, or mobility depending upon its feeding habits. Some species use the tongue to identify food by taste, others by touch. With the exception of parrots, the bulk of a bird's tongue contains no muscle. The muscles are located along the "horns" of the hyoid apparatus and extend to the skull.

A parrot's tongue, however, does have some muscles in the bulky part. This feature gives a parrot (and also parakeets) the mobility to manipulate a nut or seed within its mouth and allows the tongue to be used like a finger. The extreme extendibility of the woodpecker's tongue makes it a spear or probe for food gathering.

The tongue occupies the space in the lower mouth and generally conforms to the skeletal shape of the lower mandible. The very fleshy tongue is attached to the floor of the mouth by only a small portion of its undersurface. The cornified covering is rather thick with the tip being sharply pointed and sometimes hard and horny.

Parrots have a thick, muscular tongue that is used like a finger to manipulate food.

Compared to the size of the bill, the tongue of a skimmer is very small so that it does not get in the way when the bird is swallowing whole fish.

Tongues range in size from a tiny nodule, or sliver of flesh, to quite large, thick, and fleshy, as seen in flamingos. The size of the bill does not necessarily determine the size of the tongue. In cormorants, pelicans, skimmers, and anhingas the tongue is quite small even though the bill is rather large. These birds are fish eaters that swallow their food whole, and a large tongue would get in the way. In these birds the only purpose of the tongue is, perhaps, to cover the larynx when swallowing.

Flesh eaters, such as hawks and owls, have a rather simple tongue. The posterior end of the tongue is forked and has rather coarse, rearward projecting papillae. These backward projections of the tongue and palate are an aid when moving food to the back of the mouth to be swallowed. In the majority of smaller sized birds, the papillae are not large enough to be readily seen, and the carver need not be concerned with portraying them. In larger birds, however, such as osprey and eagles, the papillae on the tongue may be visible, and the serious carver should include this texture when portraying an open-mouthed bird.

Titmice and nuthatches have a tongue with tiny hornlike projections at the tip to aid them in gathering small insects in the crevices of tree bark. Songbirds—thrushes and warblers—have a tongue that appears to be typical of passerines. Rather thick at the posterior, or base, and slightly split, or frayed, at the tip, the songbird's tongue has very little variation.

The tongue of a hawk is basically triangular in shape with rearward pointing "horns." It also contains rasplike papillae used to hold and move food.

Hummingbirds have a specialized tongue with thin edges that curl into troughlike tubes that are frayed at the tip. Nectar and tiny insects are gathered in the troughs by capillary action while the tongue is extended, then swallowed when the tongue is retracted and the edges unfurl.

The tongues of woodpeckers are barbed at the tip and have a sticky salivary coating. Aided by extreme extendibility, the woodpecker can reach deep into crevices and holes to gather larvae and insects that stick to the barbed tip of the tongue. With respect to bill size, the woodpecker has the longest tongue of any species. In some species of woodpecker, the hyoid apparatus is four times as long as the upper mandible.

The edges of a hummingbird's tongue curl into a tubular formation when the bird gathers nectar. The fringed tip and furled edges work by capillary action.

The tip of a woodpecker's tongue has a barbed tip to help extract insects from crevices.

NINE

Senses

It is generally accepted that all animals have, to some extent, the five senses of taste, touch, smell, sight, and sound. Sight and sound, of course, are related to the eyes and ears and will not be dealt with here. The other three senses, however, are directly related to the bill and mouth. Of the three, touch is probably the most highly developed sense in the bills of all birds due to the abundant presence of Herbst and Gandry's corpuscles. Herbst corpuscles, especially, appear in great numbers in the bills and mouths of all birds. These corpuscles are highly sensitive to vibration and become a sense of touch mechanism.

It is necessary for any living animal to determine what is safe or harmful to eat. One method of distinguishing the difference between safe and harmful food is by taste. This ability to separate various flavors is present in birds as well as in mammals.

Taste buds are chemical sensory recep-tors that can distinguish the presence of acids (sourness), sugars (sweetness), alka-loids (bitterness), and salts (saltiness). Taste buds are found at the base, or poste-rior end, of the tongue and also in the softer part of the palate. Birds normally swallow their food quickly because they have no teeth for chewing and have rela-tively few taste sensors compared to other animals.

Humans have about nine thousand taste buds in the mouth, while a pigeon has fewer than seventy. A day old domes-tic chicken has only eight taste buds. Some species of parrots appear to have the highest number—nearly four hundred—of any bird. Many taste experiments have been done to determine the ability of birds to distinguish various flavors. Results seem to indicate that nearly all birds have some sense of taste, while a few species have keen responses to certain substances.

Olfactory glands, used for smell, are

located just in front of the orbital or eye cavity. Nerve endings lead into the nasal cavity where the various odors are detected. In birds with impervious nostrils, such as the cormorant, the nasal cavity opens into the buccal cavity, or mouth, and smell takes place through the mouth. The sense of smell is highly developed in some species and much less sensitive in others. The kiwi, for example, locates its food mainly by smell as do vultures and other carrion eaters.

In the soft parts of the mouth of seed-eating birds a large number of mucous glands are found. These glands moisten the food just before a bird swallows. Mucous glands are few in aquatic birds, and pelicans have none at all. Shorebirds, and many others, will moisten their food in water before they eat.

Also in the mouth there are as many as seven pairs of salivary glands. The primary purpose of salivary glands is to moisten and lubricate food before a bird swallows. These glands are poorly developed in most birds but are abundant and well developed in seed eaters. In seed-eating species, the salivary glands produce not only saliva but also a starchy enzyme to aid in digestion. Generally, birds that eat slippery foods, such as fish or frogs, have poorly developed salivary glands. Birds that eat dry types of food, such as seeds and insects, have rather well-developed salivary glands.

A few species have very special salivary glands. The woodpecker has a two-part gland with ducts that open under the tongue. One part of this special salivary gland produces a sticky fluid that coats the tongue, causing insects to stick to it. The yellow shafted flicker has a unique gland that produces an alkaline fluid used to neutralize the acid found in ants, which make up much of the bird's diet.

Probably the most unusual or unique salivary glands are those of swifts. The salivary glands of swifts produce a very sticky, gluelike secretion used to glue together the nest materials and attach them to the walls of chimneys, cliffs, or caves. At least one species of swift builds its nest entirely from the saliva secreted from an enlarged salivary gland. In the Orient these nests are collected to make bird's nest soup.

Besides taste, a bird's mouth is also sensitive to temperature. Birds will not drink water that is too warm or too cold. Experiments with domestic chickens show that the birds would rather suffer extreme thirst than drink water that was ten degrees Farenheit warmer than their body temperature.

Except in a few species, the lining of the mouth in an adult bird is a light red or pinkish color with the tongue being slightly darker in color than the rest of the mouth. Normally, the inside of the upper and lower mandibles at the tip is the same color as the outside.

TEN

Teeth

More than a hundred million years have passed since the time of Archeopteryx (Jurassic period) or Hesperornis (Cretaceous period), and birds no longer have teeth. Many species, however, have what can be construed as teeth. The tomia of mergansers, for example, have saw-toothed serrations that resemble teeth. These backward slanting serrations are bone projections of the mandible covered by a hard ramphotheca. These "teeth" of the merganser are an aid for holding the slippery fish it eats.

The lamellate bills of ducks, geese, and flamingos have a row of somewhat flexible, parallel ridges perpendicular to the tomia. These lamellations are used to strain the food from the waters in which the birds feed. Lamellations appear in several other species that feed in the water. The tomia and palate vary in shape between species. These variations are also an aid to the ornithologist when identifying or cataloging a species.

Several species of seed eaters have a hard, longitudinal ridge on the anterior (front) part of the palate. This hard keel-like ridge is an aid to cracking open seeds or nuts. The common grackle has this palatal ridge, which it uses to crack open acorns and kernels of corn.

In other seed-eating birds, the tomia on the upper mandible form a V-shaped groove with the outer margin of the palate. The tomia of the lower mandible normally rests in this groove. When eating or shelling a seed, the bird's upper and lower tomia become an efficient, three-point nutcracker.

Seed-eating birds have a hard palatal ridge that is used to crack open kernels, as seen in the bill cross sections of the goldfinch (left) and the grosbeak (right).

ELEVEN

Color

Often, the bill is the most colorful part of a bird, as seen in toucans and puffins. In most birds, however, the bill is black, but it can be almost any color or combination of colors. The bills of some species change color with the seasons. Robins have a yellow bill during breeding season, but in the fall the bill is a dark brown. Just the opposite is true of the house sparrow. The bill is black during mating season and yellowish brown in the fall. The evening grosbeak's greenish yellow bill turns bright green during mating. Puffins will molt, or shed, the bright colors of their bills after mating season.

The changing of colors on a bird, or a part of a bird, is referred to as morphism, or simply morph. When only two color morphs are involved, it is known as dimorphism; polymorphism involves several color variations. Although morphism usually refers to the plumage, it also involves the bill, eyes, legs, and feet.

Color in the ramphotheca is produced by biochromes, or pigments, found in the integument. There are three types of biochromes, or pigment colors. Melanins produce the colors of yellow, red-brown, dark brown, and black. Carotenoids, named after the pigment found in the carrot, giving it an orange color, normally produce yellow, orange, and red. The third pigment type, porphyrins, produce a fluorescent red.

Occasionally, there appears in any species the state of albinism. A bird with albinism lacks color and appears to be entirely white, and this includes the bird's legs, feet, and bill. Some birds that are normally white, such as egrets, are not albinos. Albinism is caused by the absence of pigments in the skin. There are varying degrees of albinism ranging from total albinism to partial albinism. The totally albino bird will have all white feathers, pale white legs, feet, and bill, and pinkish eyes. Totally albino birds are rarely seen in the wild.

TWELVE

Function and Use

The bills and mouths of all birds are used in many functions, but the primary function, of course, is gathering food and eating. The bill is a primary tool for any bird and is often used like a hand, and the tongue, in some cases, is used like a finger. Food gathering, however, is not done the same way in every species, and it is usually the shape of the bill that determines the manner in which a species collects its food.

The long, sharp-pointed bills of the anhinga and the Western grebe become spears for catching fish, though only a few species will spear their prey. Most often the bill is used like a pair of forceps to clamp shut on the food it gathers. In some cases this forceps' action is reversed, and the bill is used to pry apart an object. Birds with lamellate bills, such as ducks and flamingos, use their bills to strain their food from the water.

The anhinga uses its bill as a spear to catch the fish it eats.

The scissorlike tips of the crossbill are used to spread and pry open pine cones to gain access to the seeds, which are then gathered with the tongue. Many species of tree-climbing birds use their bills as reverse forceps to pry apart the bark of trees while looking for food.

The woodcock, snipe, and some other members of the sandpiper family have bills that are softer and more flexible at the tip. These birds have the ability to flex the tip of the upper mandible upward as they probe the soft earth for their meals.

Woodcocks can open the tips of their bills when probing the earth for worms. The quadrate bone is rotated to apply pressure through the zygomatic bar to bend the maxilla tip upward.

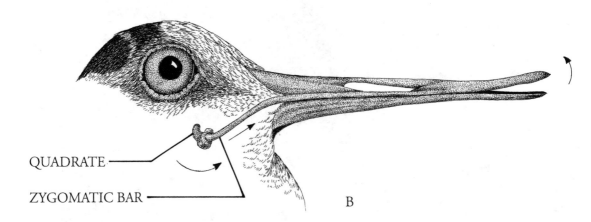

QUADRATE

ZYGOMATIC BAR

A

QUADRATE

ZYGOMATIC BAR

B

This bill flexing is possible primarily due to the skeletal structure of the upper mandible rather than by muscular action. In order to flex the tip upward, the quadrate bone is rotated causing the zygomatic bar to apply forward pressure to the tip of the bill. This forward pressure causes the tip to bend upward creating an opening while the remaining part of the bill remains closed. With the sensitive "touch receptors" in the woodcock's bill, the bird can feel when it is in contact with food. The woodcock finds its primary diet of worms by touch rather than by sight.

Turnstones were named due to the way they forage for food. The bird uses its bill to turn over small stones along the shore in order to find the small crustaceans that make up much of its diet. Pelicans make use of their gular sac to scoop up the fish they eat. This gular pouch also becomes a serving bowl to feed the young.

One of the most unusual methods of food gathering is seen in skimmers. The lower mandible of a skimmer is considerably longer than the upper mandible. The skimmer's lower mandible has a large number of Herbst corpuscles and is quite sensitive to touch. With its mouth held open, a skimmer will fly low over the water, slicing the water surface with the lower mandible. When the lower mandible comes in contact with a fish, the skimmer's head quickly moves downward and rearward. The mouth snaps shut to grasp the fish, and the head is quickly raised to swallow the prey. The tongue of a skimmer is extremely small, since it serves very little purpose in food gathering and would get in the way if it were larger. Perhaps the only purpose of a skimmer's tongue is to block the glottis while the bird is swallowing.

Some species of insect eaters will catch their food, one piece at a time, by using their bills as a pair of forceps. Other insect eaters will fly with their mouths open wide and, aided by the bristles growing around the mouth, simply net the insects. Birds that trap insects in this manner usually have a thicker, harder palate to handle the impact of the insects that strike it.

Bills are used by all birds to rid the feathers and skin of parasites and to preen the feathers. Preening is done by several methods. Usually the feather is slid between the upper and lower mandibles, causing the barbules of the feather to interlock. Nibbling of the feather with the tip of the bill is another method of preening, probably to rid the feather of parasites. Sometimes a bird will simply comb the feathers with the tip of the bill in order to arrange them.

The great flexibility of the head and neck allows a bird to reach nearly every part of its body with its bill. With this flexibility it is only logical that the bill becomes, perhaps, the most useful tool a bird possesses. Ducks, and many other species, give themselves a protective coating by brushing an oily substance onto their feathers with their bill. This substance is produced in an oil-gland located on the dorsal (top) side, near the base of the tail.

The head and bill itself are normally scratched and preened by using a foot, and there are two methods of doing this: over the wing or under the wing. Sometimes the bill is preened by rubbing it against a branch or rock. This action is known as bill-wiping. In some species, a mated pair will preen each other's head and bill. Barn owls are one species that engage in this reciprocal preening, sometimes called mutual preening.

Just as in humans, birds will stretch certain muscle groups to help relax. Bill-stretching is a relaxation movement similar to a yawn. The bills of birds are also used quite often in courtship and nuptial rituals. The act of preening one another is a common ritual, either prior to or immediately after, the act of copulation. Some species will touch or rub their bills together in a display of affection known as billing, which is somewhat akin to the holding of hands by humans. The male waxwing places his bill in the mouth of his mate, and ravens clasp each others bill in an extended kiss.

During incubation, the bill is used to move and rotate the eggs. Most species will remove the broken eggshells from the nest as soon as the infant bird has hatched. Usually the eggshell is simply dropped over the side of the nest, but some species will carry the shell in their bill away from the nest site. A few species will eat the eggshells after the young bird has hatched.

Birds are warm-blooded creatures with body temperatures that range from 98.6 degrees F., as in humans, to 113 degrees F. In humans, body temperature is regulated primarily by perspiration and evaporation. Birds do not perspire or sweat. In birds, body temperature is regulated primarily by a fluffing of the feathers, which creates varying amounts of insulation.

The bill and mouth are also used extensively for regulating body temperature. Cooling of the bird on extremely hot days is done by several methods. The respiratory, or breathing, system contains several pairs of air sacs. These air sacs are used in conjunction with panting, or taking short quick breaths. Panting with the mouth open allows moisture to evaporate, thus cooling the air as the bird breathes. This evaporative cooling method is modified somewhat in certain species. Pelicans and boobies will flutter the gular sac with the mouth open instead of panting to accomplish the same purpose.

For the carver or artist to depict a bird in extreme temperature conditions— either hot or cold—requires some consideration of attitude, position, or appearance. A bird in extreme heat, for instance, would have the feathers held close to the body to lessen the insulation. This attitude gives the bird a more sleek and slender appearance than normal. In addition, the bird would probably have its mouth open to help cool down by evaporative cooling.

Just as in mammals, a bird's first response to cold is to shiver. In extreme cold, a bird will fluff its feathers to increase insulation, have its mouth closed, and draw up the neck to place the head closer to the body. Also, most birds will squat on their feet to keep themselves warm unless their feet are already protected by a feather covering as in some owls.

Bills also become a defensive weapon during mating rituals, territory protection, or the threat of a predator. The bill of a raptor becomes an instrument of death for its prey. After catching its food with its toes, a raptor will kill the prey by biting into the vertebral column with the tip of its hooked bill. The loggerhead shrike uses its bill to impale its food on a long thorn, or a barbwire fence, to hold it in place while the bird is eating.

The bill of each species is totally adapted for the environment in which the bird lives and feeds. Each species has its own ecological niche or area of the environment in which it lives and feeds. Varying bill characteristics allow for several closely related species to survive in an area at the same time. This adaptation can readily be seen in many of the shorebirds. Turnstones and sandpipers can coexist in the same area because they forage and eat different types of food. There are six species of storks in Africa that all live and survive in the same environmental area because they forage differently. One species eats small fish while another eats larger fish. Woollyneck storks eat frogs and snakes while the marabou stork eats mostly carrion. Each has its own ecological niche.

THIRTEEN

Learning More

Every day more and more reference material is becoming available to the wildfowl carver and artist. Wildlife photographers, especially, provide the carver with much of the available reference material. A handful of photographers have specialized in providing carvers and artists with good reference photos. Photographs alone, though, are not sufficient to gather all the information necessary for reproducing a bill or a mouth.

The serious carver is constantly in search of new and better references. As the skill level of a carver progresses, so too does his or her discrimination of accurate reference material. Study skins are very good references for feather shapes, size, and sometimes color, but are not necessarily accurate reference sources for a bill. The majority of study skins available have been in existence for many years. Regardless of how well the skin has been prepared, all skins begin losing moisture and

elasticity upon the death of the bird. This moisture loss has little effect on the feathers but has great effect on the feet and bill of the bird.

Small details of the bill, such as ripples, may be lost due to shrinkage. Furthermore, the mouth is not accessible on a study skin without damaging the specimen. Even if the mouth were accessible, it would not be complete since the tongue is often removed in preparation of the skin.

Taxidermy mounts are another popular reference source but, once again, there could be shrinkage in the bill that may leave it void of some fine details. Recent taxidermy practices make use of the cast bill for many species, and it is the cast bill that gives a more accurate reference for the carver. These castings usually are made immediately after the death of a bird before any noticeable shrinkage has begun. Cast bills are available from most carving-supply houses.

A live bird is, of course, the best reference source. Unfortunately, few carvers have a private aviary stocked with the species needed. There are alternatives to this situation, however. Visits to the zoo, hikes in the forest, or just a bit of time spent in the backyard with a pair of binoculars will often provide all of the information you need.

For the serious artist, the learning process is never ending, and the more you learn about bills, the better you can portray them. I hope the material in this volume has enhanced your knowledge of a bird's bill.

Self Test

1. The bill of a bird is made up of two basic parts called the _____ and _____ .

2. The centerline ridge of the upper mandible is called the _____ .

3. The line formed where the upper and lower mandibles meet is the _____ .

4. On the tip of the upper mandibles of ducks, geese, and swans is a hard protrusion called the _____ .

5. The three basic shapes of nostril openings are _____, _____, and _____ .

6. The soft, fleshy corner of the mouth is called the _____ .

7. The ramphotheca is the _____ of the bill.

8. Birds do not have a sense of taste. (True or False)

9. The skeleton of a bird's bill contains only two bones. (True or False)

10. Soft, fleshy, extended flaps of skin growing at the corners of the mouth are called _____ .

11. The fleshy growth overlapping the nostrils on the common pigeon is called the

    _____ .

12. The cutting edges of the bill are called the _____.

13. The tongue of a bird has very little use. (True or False)

14. The buccal cavity is the correct term for the _____ .

15. When the upper mandible is longer than and curves down over the lower mandible, the bill is classed as _____ .

16. Only a few species have the ability to smell. (True or False)

17. The roof of the mouth is called the _____ .

18. The hyoid apparatus is the skeletal and muscle structure of the _____ .

19. All birds breathe through their nostrils. (True or False)

20. A parasitic bird is one that is infested with mites. (True or False)

21. Birds have no vocal cords. (True or False)

22. The pouch on the lower bill of a pelican is correctly called the _____ .

23. During extreme heat, birds keep cool by flattening the feathers against the body to reduce insulation and by _____ .

24. When there is no bone separating the two nostrils, they are said to be

    _____ .

25. The abundance of Gandry's and Herbst corpuscles in the bills of birds make them sensitive to _____ .

Answers on page 79

Glossary

Angle of the jaw. The angle formed where the mandibular ramus joins the quadrate bone.

Basihyal. The second bone from the tip of the tongue in the hyoid apparatus.

Billing. A prenuptial movement where the pair of birds will rub their bills together.

Buccal cavity. Term used for the mouth of a bird.

Ceratobranchials. In the hyoid apparatus, a pair of bones—left and right—branching off from the basihyal bone.

Cere. Similar to an operculum, but the cere is usually harder and does not overlap the nostrils, as seen in hawks and owls.

Choana. The centerline slit of the palate.

Circular. A nostril shape that is round.

Commissure. The line formed where the upper and lower mandibles meet; see also GAPE.

Cranial kinesis. Movement between the upper mandible and the skull caused by external, rather than muscle force.

Culmen. Topographically, the longitudinal centerline ridge on the upper mandible.

Dentary process. A projection of the premaxilla that forms the outer, forward part of the upper mandible.

Epibranchials. The posterior pair of bones—left and right—that are part of the hyoid apparatus.

Gape. A term used to describe an open mouth or the space between the mandibles when the mouth is open.

Glossohyal. First bone of the hyoid apparatus that is the skeleton for the bulk of the tongue.

Glottis. The slitlike opening at the lower rear of the mouth created by the laryngeal folds.

Gonys. The centerline ridge on the ventral side of the lower mandible.

Hyoid apparatus. Collectively, all the bones of the tongue.

Imperforate. When the nasal cavity is separated by a thin bony wall.

Impervious. When the nostril openings are blocked by bone or are totally absent.

Integument. The covering of a bird or animal that envelopes and protects the flesh beneath and includes the skin, hair, feathers, and scales.

Jugal. One of two bones that make up the zygomatic bar; see also QUADRATO-JUGAL.

Keratin. A protein substance in the skin used for producing feathers, scales, and the ramphotheca.

Laryngeal folds. Two fleshy flaps—left and right—at the lower rear of the mouth creating a slitlike opening; see also GLOTTIS.

Linear. A nostril shape that is slitlike, as seen in gulls.

Lower mandible. Name given to the lower half of a bird's bill.

Lower mandibular tomium. The hard, cutting edge along one side of the lower mandible. (pl. tomia)

Mandibular ramus. The "horns" of the V-shaped lower jaw.

Maxilla. A pair of bones that form part of the structure of the tomium; also, a term for upper mandible. (pl. maxillae)

Nail. A hard protrusion on the tip of the upper mandible as seen on ducks, geese, and some other species.

Nares. The openings to the nasal passage; also called nostrils.

Nasal fossa. A slight depression of the bill, at the nostrils in most songbirds.

Nasal process. Projections of the premaxilla that are fused together to form the culmen and the inner margins of the nasal passage.

Nasals. A pair of bones—left and right—that form the outer margins of the nasal cavity.

Nasal septum. Thin, platelike, longitudinal bone that divides the nostril openings.

Nostrils. Opening in the bill through which air passes for breathing; see also NARES.

Operculate. Referring to a bill that has an operculum.

Operculum. Latin for lid; this is a rather soft, fleshy growth overlapping the nostrils, as seen on the common pigeon.

Oval. A nostril shape that is elliptical or teardrop in shape.

Palatal folds. The left and right halves of the palate; see also CHOANA.

Palatal process. Projections of the premaxilla that are fused along their centerline to form the front portion of the palate.

Palate. The roof of the mouth.

Palatines. A pair of bones—left and right—that forms the roof of the mouth.

Perforate. Not having a nasal septum.

Pharyngeal folds. Small, membranous flaps at the entrance to the pharynx, usually having tiny, backward-slanting papillae.

Pharynx. Located posterior to the palate, this is the opening into the digestive tract.

Premaxilla. One of a pair of bones—left and right—that are fused together to form the tip of the bill. (pl. premaxillae)

Pterygoids. A pair of bones in the skull that form an articulated joint with the palatine bones.

Quadrate. A bone of the skull having four points of articulation. Where the quadrate joins the lower mandible is the ANGLE OF THE JAW.

Quadratojugal. One of two bones that make up the zygomatic bar; see also JUGAL.

Ramphotheca. That part of the integument covering the ramus, or bill.

Ramus. Collectively the upper and lower mandibles; the bill.

Rictus. The soft, fleshy corners of the mouth that complete the tomium.

Salivary glands. Glands in the mouth that secrete moisture and enzymes.

Syrinx. Located at the lower end of the trachea, this is the voice box of birds.

Taste buds. Glands in the mouth that are sensitive to chemical compositions such as sweet, sour, and so on.

Tomium. The perimeter edges of either the upper or lower mandibles.

Tomium proper. The hard, cutting edge of the tomium; see also RICTUS.

Upper mandible. Name given to the upper half of a bird's bill; see also MAXILLA.

Upper mandibular tomium. The hard, cutting edge along one side of the upper mandible.

Ventral process. An inward and downward projection at the posterior end of the maxillae bone. The ventral process in humans forms the support for the teeth in the upper jaw.

Zygomatic bar. The long slender bone on either side of the upper mandible that joins the quadrate; made up of the fused jugal and quadratojugal.

Bibliography

Although a great number of sources were used as reference material for this book, the primary sources were as follows:

Brooke, M., and T. Birkhead, eds. *Cambridge Encyclopedia of Ornithology*. New York: Cambridge Press, 1991.

Farner, D. S., J. R. King Jr., and K. C. Parke, eds. *Avian Biology*. 2 vols. New York: Academic Press, 1971.

Pasquier, Roger F. *Watching Birds: An Introduction to Ornithology*. Boston: Houghton Mifflin Co., 1977.

Peterson, Roger Tory. *The Birds*. (Life Nature Library). New York: Time Inc., 1963.

Pettingill, O. S., Jr. *Ornithology in Laboratory and Field*. Orlando, Fla.: Academic Press, 1985.

Sturkie, Paul D. *Avian Physiology*. Ithaca, N. Y.: Cornell University Press, 1965.

Terres, J. K. *Encyclopedia of North American Birds*. New York: Wings Books, 1991.

VanTyne, J. and A. J. Berger. *Fundamentals of Ornithology*. New York: Dover Publications, 1971.

Wilson, Barry W. *Birds, Readings from Scientific American*. New York: W. H. Freeman Co., 1980.

TEST ANSWERS

1. Upper mandible and lower mandible

2. Culmen

3. Commissure

4. Nail or unguis

5. Linear, or slitlike; round, or circular; oval, or teardrop

6. Rictus

7. Integument or covering

8. False. Nearly all birds have some sense of taste.

9. False. There are more than two dozen separate bones that make up the skeleton of the bill.

10. Lappets or rictal wattles

11. Operculum

12. Tomia

13. False. The tongue is often used as a "finger" to manipulate food on the mouth or to gather food.

14 Mouth

15. Hooked

16. False. All birds have a sense of smell.

17. Palate

18. Tongue

19. False. Birds with impervious nostrils must breathe through the mouth.

20. False. A parasitic species lays its eggs in the nest of another species.

21. True. Bird sounds are produced in the syrinx.

22. Gular sac

23. Panting, gular flutter, or evaporative cooling

24. Perforate

25. Touch

ABOUT THE AUTHOR

Jack Kochan is a veteran bird carver whose interest in the hobby was sparked ten years ago by a visit to a decoy factory. Since then his carvings have earned numeous awards, including first-place honors at the Ward World Championships in 1990. He credits his success to his knowledge of avian anatomy, which he says helps him create detailed, lifelike carvings. As an artist and illustrator, Kochan has produced work for a variety of publications. An avid outdoorsman, he lives in Leesport, Pennsylvania.

The Bird Carving Basics Series
by Curtis J. Badger

This series offers world-class carving tips at a reasonable price. Each volume presents a variety of techniques from carvers like Jim Sprankle, Leo Osborne, Martin Gates, and Floyd Scholz. Illustrated with exceptional step-by-step photos.

The eleven volume series:

Eyes

Feet

Habitat

Tools

Heads

Bills and Beaks

Texturing

Painting

Special Painting Techniques

Songbird Painting

How to Compete

For complete ordering information, write:

STACKPOLE
BOOKS

5067 Ritter Road
Mechanicsburg, PA 17055
or call 1-800-732-3669